understanding
Jung

Ruth Snowden

flash.

For UK order enquiries: please contact Bookpoint Ltd,
130 Milton Park, Abingdon, Oxon OX14 4SB.
Telephone: +44 (0) 1235 827720. *Fax:* +44 (0) 1235 400454.
Lines are open 09.00–17.00, Monday to Saturday, with a 24-hour
message answering service. Details about our titles and how to
order are available at www.hoddereducation.com

British Library Cataloguing in Publication Data: a catalogue record for
this title is available from the British Library.

First published in UK 2011 by Hodder Education, part of Hachette UK,
338 Euston Road, London NW1 3BH.

Typeset by MPS Limited, a Macmillan Company.

Printed in Great Britain for Hodder Education, an Hachette UK Company,
338 Euston Road, London NW1 3BH, by CPI Cox & Wyman, Reading,
Berkshire RG1 8EX.

The publisher has used its best endeavours to ensure that the URLs for
external websites referred to in this book are correct and active at the time of
going to press. However, the publisher and the author have no responsibility
for the websites and can make no guarantee that a site will remain live or
that the content will remain relevant, decent or appropriate.

Hachette UK's policy is to use papers that are natural, renewable and recyclable
products and made from wood grown in sustainable forests. The logging and
manufacturing processes are expected to conform to the environmental
regulations of the country of origin.

Impression number   10 9 8 7 6 5 4 3 2 1
Year   2015 2014 2013 2012 2011

Contents

Introduction

Who was Jung?

Carl Jung (1875–1961) was a Swiss psychologist and psychiatrist. He is famous because he founded a new system of psychology that he called 'analytical psychology'. Jung has gradually acquired a huge following and many therapists today are trained in methods that have their roots in Jung's work.

Jung was a prolific writer and he had a wide range of interests, covering such areas as astrology, alchemy, archaeology and world religions. The system of psychology that he developed was very much a spiritual psychology, marking it apart from the mainstream, which tended to be rigidly 'mechanistic' in outlook. People were seen as machines, with their behaviour determined by physical or chemical causes. Jung explored many spiritual traditions, believing a person's spiritual life to be crucial in the healing process. For Jung, a person's life story was what mattered – he regarded clinical diagnoses as being useful to the doctor, rather than helpful to the patient.

Jung was born towards the end of the nineteenth century, at a time when great changes were beginning to take place in society, particularly in the field of science. People were searching for new truths and becoming more interested in self-knowledge: Charles Darwin's theory of evolution had made people question the truth of the Bible, and Sigmund Freud was expanding people's awareness of the unconscious. Jung insisted that the psyche is no less real than the physical world. He pointed out that everything that we are aware of is perceived and interpreted by the brain, so that we can never know for certain the truth about the outside world.

What is analytical psychology?

Analytical psychology is a whole system of psychology that Jung gradually developed throughout his life. His ideas came from nearly 60 years of experience as a practising psychologist.

He studied the experiences of his patients and his own inner world and its dreams, visions and symbols. Throughout his life he read and travelled widely, and found that certain common themes ran through the myths and culture of all people. This led to his idea of the 'collective unconscious' – the deepest layer of the unconscious, extending beyond the individual psyche. This is one of the central themes in Jungian teaching.

Analytical psychology has several main aspects. It is:

* a method of therapy, aimed at treating mental and nervous disorders, and also at helping ordinary people to become more balanced and self-aware;
* an attempt to provide a map of the human psyche in order to understand more fully how it works.
* an exploration of the deeper aspects of human psychology through the study of religious beliefs, dreams, myths, symbols and the paranormal.

1

Jung's life and career

Jung was greatly influenced by his rural and religious upbringing and saw the spiritual aspects of his work as being the most important. For him the hidden world of the psyche was as real as the external world. He came to realize that the integration of the different facets of the personality is a very important life task, and the goal of analytical psychology. Jung studied medicine at university, then specialized in psychiatry. He called his new system of psychology 'analytical psychology' in order to distinguish it from 'psychoanalysis', developed by Sigmund Freud, who was initially his mentor.

Jung was often regarded as an eccentric, especially by more orthodox scientists. But he was charismatic and gradually acquired a huge following, eventually becoming world renowned. He was usually cheerful and outgoing, but could be moody and difficult to live with.

Jung's family background

Jung was born on 26 July 1875 in Kesswil, a small village in Switzerland on the shores of Lake Constance. He was the second child born to his parents, but their first born had died soon after birth. When he was six months old, Jung's family moved to another village called Laufen, close to the border with Germany and France and near the great Falls of the Rhine. Then they moved again, this time to Klein-Hüningen, which was at that time just a village, near Basel, also located on the Rhine.

The little villages in which Jung was born and raised had a huge influence on him that was to last throughout his life. It was a peaceful, rural world of mountains and lakes, rocks, rivers and abundant wildlife. His earliest memory is one of lying in a pram, under the shadow of a tree on a warm summer's day, and feeling a great sense of glorious beauty and indescribable well-being on seeing the sunlight glittering through the leaves and blossoms. Jung developed an intense love of the natural world and a deep spiritual relationship with all living things. He loved the peace and solitude that living in nature can bring, and spent a lot of time alone thinking, writing, contemplating, and finding his own inner peace. His deep connection with the earth element was also expressed in painting pictures and working with wood and stone. Animals were very important to him – he always liked to have dogs as companions, and he frequently wrote of synchronous messages that came to him from the natural world.

When Jung was nine, his sister Gertrude was born, but she played little part in his childhood. The age gap between them was too great and their temperaments were very different. Young Carl was already a solitary child and liked to play alone, lost in his own inner world. Gertrude was delicate and died quite young. Jung said that she was always a stranger to him, and that where he was emotional she was always very composed, although she was very sensitive deep down.

Jung had many relations in the Church – eight of his uncles were pastors. His father was a pastor in the Swiss Reformed Church, whose teachings were strongly influenced by the sixteenth century Reformation teachings of leaders such as Calvin and Luther. The Reformed Church taught people to believe in the literal truth of the Bible, or else risk damnation. Jung's father had strong scholarly interests in classical and Oriental studies, but he accepted the teachings of his church without question. Jung said later in life that in childhood he associated the word 'father' with reliability, but also with weakness.

Jung's mother was also rooted in the faith of the Reformed Church. However, her beliefs were more complex because her own family firmly believed in contact with the spirit world. Old pagan beliefs still held strong in the minds of people in rural Switzerland. Jung saw his mother as a dynamic and powerful person, but also as unpredictable and mysterious. His parents' marriage was not an easy one, probably because their characters and beliefs were so different. His mother was earthy, extrovert and chatty, whereas his father was scholarly and introvert. When Jung was three, his mother was hospitalized for several months with a nervous illness. When he was nine, his sister Gertrude was born, but she died at a young age and played little part in his childhood. Young Carl was a solitary child and liked to play alone.

The different influences from his parents probably played a part in creating a dualism that Jung recognized in himself later in life. He felt that his personality was divided into two characters which he called 'Number 1' and 'Number 2'.

* Number 1 was concerned with the external everyday world. This side of Jung was ambitious and analytical, looking at the world from a scientific point of view.
* Number 2 was secretive and mysterious and tended to look at things in an intuitive way.

A brief outline of Jung's career

School

Jung attended a country school where he was intellectually well ahead of his classmates. He welcomed the company of other children, but close friendships were not easy for him because he was so used to playing alone. From the age of 11 he attended a school in Basel, but he was never happy there. The other boys thought him peculiar and tended to make fun of him. Not only that, but he found the lessons boring and felt that they were a waste of his time.

University

Family poverty meant that Jung could not expect to study at a more distant university, so he was admitted to Basel in 1895 after leaving school. He had wanted to study archaeology but it was not taught at Basel, so he chose medicine instead. This was in the family already; his paternal grandfather was Professor of Surgery at the university until 1864. After taking his degree in medicine in 1900, Jung almost decided to specialize in surgery, but he had developed a strong interest in psychiatry and eventually decided to move in this direction. He realized that this was the best way to combine his scientific interests with his interests in religion and the paranormal.

First appointments

Jung became an assistant at the Burghölzli mental hospital in 1900, and in 1905 he was appointed Lecturer in Psychiatry at Zürich University. He was especially interested in the disorder then called dementia praecox, later known as schizophrenia. Jung left the hospital in 1909, so that he could work with private patients. He also wanted to concentrate on his research into the psychological aspects of behaviour and the inner world of the unconscious.

Recognition of his importance

In 1907 Jung met Sigmund Freud and for a number of years they had a close friendship. Jung became the first president of Freud's International Psychoanalytic Society and was the editor of its journal, which was the first of its kind. Eventually Jung's independent way of thinking led to a rift with Freud. He continued to develop his own school of psychology and he was made president of the International General Medical Society for Psychotherapy in 1933. In 1936, when Harvard University marked its tercentenary by awarding honorary degrees to the most eminent living scientists, Jung was one of the people chosen for the honour. His reputation had grown and he had become a leader of international research work in psychology, partly because he eagerly exchanged ideas with others. Even in old age he was known as a great conversationalist who retained a wide range of information about different topics. His charismatic personality meant that he attracted a huge following.

Jung's private life

Jung met his wife, Emma Rauschenbach, when he was 21 and she was 16. The first time they met she was standing at the top of a staircase, and Jung had an immediate premonition that she was to be his wife. They were married seven years later, in 1903, and their first child Agathe was born in 1904. Over the next ten years they had four more children – three girls and a boy. At first they lived in rooms at the Burghölzli hospital, but in 1909 they were able to move into a newly built house on the lakeside at Kusnacht near Zürich. Jung had known from very early childhood that he wanted to live near a lake. Luckily for him, Emma was the daughter of a wealthy businessman, and this left Jung free to pursue his own interests a lot of the time.

Emma Jung worked as an analyst in the therapy practice, taking on her own patients. She also gave lectures at the Jungian institute in Zürich. She was especially interested in Arthurian legends, and made a special study of the legend of the Holy Grail. Antonia Wolff also worked alongside Jung and became his mistress from around 1911 onwards. The relationship became a complex triangular one. Jung announced that a man needed two women: one to organize the domestic affairs and one to stimulate the intellect. He was an incurable womanizer and had many other affairs in addition to his relationship with Antonia.

Jung outlived both his beloved women and missed them in his last years. He carved memorial stones for each of them, with Chinese inscriptions. Emma's reads 'she was the foundation of my house' and Antonia's 'she was the fragrance of the house'. He did not write a great deal about people who were close to him, probably in order to protect them.

Jung travelled extensively, visiting North Africa, New Mexico, Kenya, Uganda and India. He lectured in both Britain and the US. People usually described Jung as being friendly and interested, but he had odd moods when he would become preoccupied, even rude. At these times he would withdraw from society and he built a special retreat at Bollingen for this purpose. When the mood took him, he was driven by the need to indulge in creative activity or study. This meant that he sometimes hurt people or made enemies because he appeared distant.

Jung died in 1961 after a brief illness. Since his death, his analysis of the human psyche has been widely recognized as an important framework for studying psychological problems. By his own admission, his ideas are not always easy to follow, but he certainly encouraged people to experience things for themselves and develop their own insights. Near the end of his life he tried to put some of his main ideas together in a way that was more understandable to ordinary people. The result was a book called *Man and his Symbols*, which makes a good starting point for studying Jung's ideas. The book emphasizes Jung's lifelong conviction that the inner world of the human psyche is of paramount importance and needs to be studied seriously.

2

Jung's early life

Jung was a solitary, introspective child and in his imaginative games he explored his inner world and began to grapple with ideas that were to fascinate him all his life. School largely bored him and it was not until he discovered psychiatry that he began to find his true path. The differences in outlook between his parents led to duality and conflict in Jung's psyche. He was an independent thinker and throughout his life his deep interest in the spiritual had profound influences on his work.

Jung studied medicine at university and then specialized in psychiatry, working with psychotic patients. This experience inspired an interest in personality development and he realized that a person's symptoms often make sense in the light of their individual story. Sigmund Freud was an important early influence on Jung but differences in their thinking, especially about the nature of the unconscious, led to a rift between them.

Boyhood

Because Jung played alone a great deal when he was a child, he became introspective and developed a rich and imaginative inner world. His later work as an analyst and a great thinker had its roots here. Young Carl spent a lot of time pondering over philosophical and religious questions, many of which were very sophisticated for his age. His country playmates were fun to be with, but he felt that they alienated him from his true self – he was only able to be truly himself when he played alone. Later in life he remarked that he felt he needed people both more and less than others did. He found people fascinating, but he also needed a lot of personal space.

In his autobiographical book *Memories, Dreams, Reflections*, written towards the end of his life, Jung recalls various important incidents from his childhood. Some of these were to have profound effects and haunt him all his life, as detailed below.

The stone

When he was aged between seven and nine, Jung played often near a wall made of large blocks of stone. He had a fascination for starting little fires in hollows in this wall. The fires were in some way sacred, and had to be kept fed so that they would burn forever. In front of the wall was a slope with a stone in it that jutted out so that you could sit on it. Jung would play a game where he would alternate between being himself sitting on the stone, and being the stone that was being sat on. After a while he would become uncertain of reality and would stand up wondering 'who was what now'. This confusion was exciting and interesting, and was always accompanied by 'a feeling of curious and fascinating darkness'. This was one of his first experiences of the numinous (awe-inspiring, indicating divine presence), which was to become of paramount importance to him in later years. The stone, in fact, was to become one of the foundations of his analytical psychology.

The secret manikin

When he was about ten, Jung carved a 5 cm manikin from the end of a ruler. The manikin wore a frock coat, top hat and shiny black boots. Jung made him a home in a wooden pencil case, complete with a little bed for him to lie on. He added a smooth black stone from the Rhine River, which he painted to divide it into upper and lower halves. The manikin and his sacred stone were secret and Jung hid them on a beam in the attic, where he was forbidden to play because the floorboards were unsafe.

Whenever he was upset or there was an undercurrent of trouble between his parents, Jung would sneak up to look at the manikin. Each time he visited, he added a tiny scroll, written in a secret language and bearing an important message. The secret manikin and the stone gave him a sense of power and security that was so important that he considered them to be the 'essential factor' of his boyhood. He knew that they represented an enormously important secret and this was his first real attempt to give shape to it.

Jung saw his whole life as an unfolding of 'the self-realization of the unconscious'. He felt that what he referred to as a person's 'personal myth' could express that person's inner world more precisely than science ever could. The manikin in the attic was somehow symbolic of his own inner world as a child – it was a part of his own evolving personal myth. Although in old age Jung's recollections of the external world had faded, his encounters with the 'other reality' were as vivid as ever. These were what really mattered to him and he seems to have been aware of this fact from an early age.

Jung's earliest recollected dream

When he was three or four, Jung dreamed that he was in a meadow, where he came across a dark stone-lined hole with steps leading down underground. He went down and there, in an underground chamber, was a wonderful golden throne. Seated on this throne was a huge thing made of flesh, 4.5–5.5 metres high and about half a metre thick. On top it had a rounded head, with a single eye gazing upwards. He was paralysed with terror and as he stood transfixed he heard his mother's voice telling him 'that is the man-eater'.

It was only years later that he realized that the thing had been a phallus. The dream was oddly un-childlike and sophisticated – where had the anatomically correct phallus, sitting like some subterranean god come from? It was not until he was about 50 years old that he connected it with a book he read about the motif of cannibalism underlying the symbolism of the Mass. He was puzzled as to how a child could have had knowledge of things that were to fill his later years with 'stormiest passion'. Jung maintained that his intellectual life had its unconscious beginnings when he had that dream.

Jung's first experience of a neurosis

Jung describes having an early personal insight into the process of forming a neurosis. When he was 12 years old he was pushed over by another boy and banged his head. After that he began to have fainting fits whenever school or work were mentioned. He was kept off school for six months and enjoyed rambling around alone, living with nature and communing with his inner world. All the while his pleasure was somewhat spoilt by a vague sense of guilt. Eventually he overheard his father talking to a friend and telling him how worried he was about his son's future. Jung rushed off and began to study his Latin books, struggling every few minutes to overcome giddy spells. Within a few weeks he was back at school and had the uncomfortable realization that he had engineered the whole thing himself. From then on he worked hard. As he walked to school one day he suddenly felt as if he had emerged from a dense cloud. He thought to himself 'now I am *myself*'.

Education

Jung was nevertheless bored by school, feeling that it took up too much of his valuable time. Many subjects he found almost too easy and did very well in them. However, he objected strongly to algebra and found maths as a whole to be 'sheer terror and torture'. Divinity he found 'unspeakably dull', despite his interest in religious questions. He had an 'utter incapacity' for drawing, and gymnastics was ruined for him by physical timidity and the fact that he resented people telling him how to move. Meanwhile, as he was growing up he had an enduring sense of inferiority, feeling himself to be somehow contemptible.

Jung was largely unpopular with his schoolmates, who thought him to be superior and a swot. He struggled with the feeling of an inner split in his personality, which seemed to force him to try and live in two very different worlds at once. Partly because of this he felt unable to decide what to study at university. Eventually he won a scholarship to study medicine at Basel University. Being at university made Jung feel alive and he made plenty of friends. He read books on philosophy as well as medicine, and he joined the university debating society where they discussed the human soul and other religious questions.

Jung felt a great wave of excitement when he first came across a book called *Text-book of Psychiatry*, by Richard von Krafft-Ebing. Krafft-Ebing spoke of the subjective nature of psychiatry, describing how the psychiatrist studied his patient with the whole of his own personality. Jung realized with a flash of illumination that here, at last, was a way in which he could integrate the two currents of his internal world. This was where science and the spiritual met.

Jung's interest in spiritualism

While he was at university Jung found a small book on spiritualism and realized that the phenomena described were related to stories that were familiar from his country childhood. Such things as predictive dreams, clocks that stopped at the moment of death, ghosts and table turning fascinated him. His friends on the other hand reacted either with total disbelief or with defensiveness, even dread.

When he was home for the summer holidays an incident occurred that affected Jung profoundly. The family heard a loud crack from the dining room. Rushing through they found that their circular walnut dining table had split right across, not along a joint, but clean through the solid wood. A few weeks later another deafening cracking sound was traced to a bread knife, which lay inside the sideboard shattered into several pieces along the blade. The knife had been used at teatime and then put away as normal.

Jung and his mother both felt that there must be some underlying reason for these two strange incidents. A few weeks later he was asked to attend a séance and he decided to go along, thinking that the incidents might be somehow to do with the medium. After that he attended regular seances on Saturday evenings. The medium, who was a young cousin of Jung's, took on the personality of a woman called Ivenes. Through Ivenes she re-lived past life experiences and dramatic love affairs. Eventually Jung lost interest when he discovered that the girl had cooked up some of the evidence in order to impress him. But he felt that the whole experience had been important because it had further aroused his interest in the human psyche.

Scientific thinking at the turn of the century

In the 1890s, when Jung was a student, psychiatry was in its infancy. People tended to see it as being related to psychical research and spiritualist ideas. These were very much in vogue at the time, and the Society for Psychical Research had been founded in 1882, in Cambridge. At the same time new scientific understanding of the unconscious was beginning to emerge, pioneered by Sigmund Freud.

The accepted way of thinking in science followed the rules of 'positivism', which limits knowledge to things that are directly observable. This approach goes hand in hand with the mechanistic view. The idea behind positivism is straightforward – you simply describe the facts of what you can experience and observe. Anything else is not considered to be science. Positivists also try to make general scientific laws about the ways in which phenomena are related. This approach began in the natural sciences and spread into philosophy. Most psychologists took a positivist stance; meanwhile, psychiatry was also developing, as people became interested in mental illnesses. It was hard to explain these illnesses by means of conventional medicine and mechanistic thinking.

Burghölzli

In 1900, Jung was appointed as an assistant at Burghölzli, a psychiatric clinic at the University of Zurich, run by Eugen Bleuler. The patients at Burghölzli were mainly psychotic (suffering from severe mental disorder). Jung worked here for nine years, studying schizophrenic illnesses. The mechanistic outlook said that such illnesses were caused by neurological damage or organic disease. However, Freud's new ideas about the unconscious were beginning to take effect, suggesting that this might not necessarily be the case. Jung was especially interested in experimental psychology and did extensive work using word tests, whereby the doctor gave the patient a word and the patient responded with whatever came first into his or her head. If a noticeable delay occurred then unconscious emotions were probably at work. Jung carefully noted reaction times and responses and found that he could identify 'complexes' of related responses. (In psychology, a 'complex' is a related group of emotionally charged, unconscious ideas.)

In 1905 Jung was appointed as a senior doctor and lecturer in the medical faculty at the university. He began to move away from experimental psychology because he felt that doctors were too keen on describing symptoms, making a diagnosis and compiling statistics – all manifestations of the mechanistic view. Jung wanted to find out what was going on in the minds of the mentally ill – he was not interested in labelling people. He pointed out that a person's crazy symptoms will often make perfect sense in the light of their individual story. The problem is always the whole person, never the symptom alone. Jung began to explore the unconscious minds of his patients, using word association or dream analysis, or simply by endlessly and patiently talking. This is where his friendship with Freud became very important.

Jung and Freud

In 1906 Jung sent an account of some of his findings to Freud, whose work on the unconscious interested him and seemed to confirm some of his findings. Freud's psychoanalytic therapy was aimed at treating mental and nervous disorders. It worked with theories about the unconscious and the ways in which it interacts with the conscious mind. The therapy was based partly on a free association process very similar to Jung's work with word association. Freud also worked a great deal with dreams and this aspect of his work also interested Jung.

Freud and Jung got on especially well at first and a kind of father–son relationship developed between them, Freud being nearly 20 years older than Jung. Freud wanted Jung to be his successor and in 1910 he appointed him as the President of the newly formed International Psychoanalytic Society in Vienna. However, problems soon began to arise in their relationship and Jung gradually began to develop new theories of his own. By 1912, Jung was still outwardly struggling to be supportive towards Freud, but he ended up criticizing the basic theories of psychoanalysis.

Jung coined the phrase 'analytical psychology' to describe the new ideas that he was evolving and to distinguish them from psychoanalysis. Letters between Freud and Jung became increasingly bitter and sadly, in 1913, their friendship ceased altogether. Although the relationship between Jung and Freud did eventually end, there is no doubt that Freud was very important in helping Jung to formulate his theories.

3

Jung's inner world

After his rift with Freud, Jung went through a long period of depression, withdrawing into his own inner world. He found that his troubled dreams and visions were connected to ideas expressed in myths, and so he began to develop his theories about the collective unconscious and 'archetypes' (recurring images or patterns of thinking which represent typical human experiences).

During his crisis Jung discovered creative play as a way of unlocking the unconscious. This was to become a very important aspect of Jungian analysis – for example, patients are often encouraged to create artwork based on dream imagery. He became fascinated by drawing symbolic, circular designs called 'mandalas' to map his progress on his journey of self-discovery. He also worked with dreams, visions and fantasies, finding that these often gave insight into a person's inner world. Dream encounters with archetypal figures were particularly important because they gave form to unconscious ideas.

Jung's midlife crisis

Jung's lengthy depression might nowadays be called a midlife crisis. He was 39, many of his former friends turned their backs on him, and he gave up his university post. He felt a great sense of disorientation, and seemed to live under a constant inner pressure. His reaction was to turn away from the world for a while and withdraw into his own inner world. Dreams and fantasies became increasingly interesting to him, not only his own, but also those of his patients. He could not understand why other doctors were so obsessed with making firm diagnoses and did not seem interested in what their patients had to say.

During his time working at Burghölzli, Jung had begun to realize that many myth-like themes emerged in the dreams and fantasies of the insane. He began to wonder whether it was possible that people carried little snippets of inherited impressions and imagery, stored in myth-like forms. From this idea he began to develop his theories about the collective unconscious and archetypes, and he began to study his own crisis almost as if he were both patient and doctor at the same time. He found references in mythology to heroes who went off on a 'Nekyia', or 'night-sea journey'. This was a very dangerous quest where the hero was likely to be swallowed up by enormous sea monsters or by an all-devouring female, before achieving re-birth. This mythical idea corresponded very closely to what was going on in Jung's own inner crisis.

Such imaginative ideas are everywhere but, as Jung had already discovered, they are often treated with dread and suspicion when they emerge into consciousness. Indeed, Jung knew all too well from his clinical work how dangerous the unconscious could be, and at times he feared that he might become psychotic like his patients. He found that his family and his work acted as anchors, preventing him from becoming totally ungrounded. However, he still felt lost, without a frame of reference, so began to look around for ways to chart his journey.

Creative play

Jung tried going over all the details of his childhood in order to try and find a cause for his disturbances. He did this twice over, but it seemed to get him nowhere. In the end he decided that the only thing to do was to be less analytical and try submitting to the impulses of his own unconscious. This had interesting results. The first thing that came into his head was a memory of a passionate interest he had had when he was about ten or eleven years old. He had used building blocks to construct little houses, castles and villages. As this memory welled up he felt very emotional and excited, so he decided to re-enact the childish phase by indulging in similar games. This felt silly at first, but he soon found that it was a good way of getting back in touch with the true essence of himself at that age.

Jung made cottages, a castle, a village and a church. Then one day, walking by the lake, he found a perfect little red stone pyramid, about 4 cm high. He was delighted, realizing that this must be the altar for his church. As he put it in position he was reminded of the phallus dream he had had when he was very little – the strange god seated on his underground throne. He felt immensely satisfied by this.

Every afternoon Jung would play until his patients arrived, and then again in the evening. For the rest of his life he used such creative play as an invaluable therapeutic tool. Whenever he came up against a mental block, he would paint or work at stone carving, and he always found that his ideas would start flowing again. Creative play was also to become a very important aspect of Jungian analysis.

Dreams, visions and fantasies

Jung found that patients would often report their dreams and fantasies to him spontaneously and he would then ask them questions, such as 'Where does that come from?' 'How does it make you feel?' Interpretations of the dreams and fantasies seemed to follow of their own accord from the patients' own replies and associations. Once again, Jung deliberately avoided all theoretical rules – he simply tried to help people to understand their own imagery.

Meanwhile, he was also fascinated by his own dreams and he spent a lot of time trying to interpret them, although this was sometimes very difficult. For example, he dreamed of a long row of corpses, each dressed in different clothes going back through the ages right to a twelfth century crusader dressed in chain mail. Each corpse in turn stirred and began to come to life as he looked at it. Jung realized that this particular dream was speaking to him about aspects of the unconscious that are handed down from the ancestors and can still stir and come to life in our own psyches. This dream tied in with the ideas that he was developing about archetypes and the collective unconscious.

In 1913, Jung began to feel as though 'there were something in the air'. The whole atmosphere seemed darker, as if his inner oppression was becoming a concrete reality. During a journey he had an overpowering vision of a huge flood that rose up and covered the whole of northern Europe. The mountains rose higher to protect Switzerland, but all around he saw the rubble of civilization and drowned bodies in a vast sea that turned to blood. The whole vision lasted an hour and made him feel quite ill. Two weeks later it returned, with even more intensity.

This gruesome experience was followed by a recurring dream that began in the spring of 1914. In his dream, Jung saw the land frozen to ice in summer time. World War I broke out in August, and Jung knew then that he had to try to understand what had happened and how his own inner experiences had coincided with the outer experiences of mankind. He realized that the only way to approach this question was to begin to carefully record and study his own fantasies and dreams. A huge stream of fantasies began to be released and he felt as if he was enduring an endless series of inner thunderstorms. He knew that he was strong, however, and that he had to find meaning in it all, not only for his own sake, but also for his patients, so that he might better understand their problems.

Discovering archetypes

Jung found that as he wrote he was often using 'high flown language'. He found this pomposity rather embarrassing, and often felt strong resistance to his fantasies, but he tried to treat the whole thing as a sort of scientific experiment. He knew all too well the dangers of becoming prey to his own fantasies, and how easy it would be to slide into psychosis.

In one vision he met a beautiful young girl, accompanied by an old man with a beard. These figures were examples of what Jung called 'archetypes' – the recurring images or patterns of thinking which form the basic content of religion, myth, art and legend. Archetypes are part of the collective unconscious and they emerge in the individual psyche through dreams and visions. Jung felt that the old man in his vision corresponded to Elijah, an Old Testament prophet, and the young girl to Salome, the archetypal seductress found in the New Testament.

After a while Jung met another archetypal figure – Philemon, a pagan sage, with the horns of a bull and the wings of a kingfisher. He carried a bunch of four keys, one of which he held as if ready to open a lock. Jung painted a picture of this apparition and shortly afterwards found a dead kingfisher in his garden by the lakeshore. This was most odd, as kingfishers were rare in the area. Jung saw the incident as providing a crucial insight that there are things in the psyche that we do not produce – they produce themselves and have their own life.

Philemon became an important guru to Jung; he began to have lengthy conversations with him, and even went for walks with him in the garden. Philemon explained to Jung that we do not generate our own thoughts: they have an external reality of their own, just like birds in the air, or people in a room. Jung realized that there was something within him that could talk about matters that he did not consciously know about, and might even act against him. Archetypal encounters were very important because they enabled Jung to give a personal form to aspects of his unconscious. Because they were in some way 'separate' from himself he was able to bring them into relationship with his conscious mind and not get too bogged down in some of their more disturbing utterances.

In 1916, a restless, ominous atmosphere was beginning to gather in Jung's home. The children took to seeing white figures at night, and had their blankets snatched away from them in bed. The doorbell rang frantically all by itself when there was nobody there, and the whole house felt thick with spirits. Eventually a whole host of them infiltrated the house and Jung began to write a book, *Septem Sermones* (Seven Sermons), which represented an exteriorization of everything in his turbulent mind. He wrote for three days and then the spirits all vanished from the house and the weird haunting was over. Jung suggests that they were parapsychological phenomena, somehow caused by his own highly charged emotional state.

Mandalas

Towards the end of World War I, Jung began to emerge from his great darkness. A major event at this time was his discovery of the *mandala*. The word *mandala* comes from Sanskrit and means 'magical circle'. The mandala is an archetypal symbol, found in many religions and in other aspects of many cultures. It is often used as a centring device to help with meditation exercises. A basic mandala is a circle containing a square or other symmetrical figure, but there are many variations. The image may represent the universe itself, or the 'inner universe' – the wholeness of the psyche. Every morning Jung did a small circular drawing of this type and observed the ways in which the drawings changed from day to day. He found that they helped him to observe his own psychic transformations – the ever-changing state of his inner world.

Jung found that his mandala drawings linked up with external experiences in his everyday life and also with his dreams. He gradually came to understand that they represented the way in which all paths in the psyche led eventually to a mid point, which is the core or essence of what he called the Self. (The capital letter distinguishes it from the more mundane meaning of the word.)

The goal of psychic development is the discovery of this unique Self. This process is what Jung called 'individuation' and it is one of the core concepts of analytical psychology. Like the mandala, the evolution of the psyche is not linear, but a process of circling around the Self. From Jung's mandala work emerged inklings of his own personal myth, his all-important 'story' that expressed his real being.

The tower at Bollingen

Jung felt that he was gradually able to put his dreams and fantasies onto a more solid footing and began to understand the unconscious in more scientific terms. He also wanted to make a representation of his innermost thoughts and knowledge in a more permanent solid way than simply writing them down on paper. For this purpose of self-expression, and also as a quiet retreat, he built his tower at Bollingen in 1922. He had a special resting room within the tower where only he was allowed to go. Here he did paintings on the walls and found that he could truly be himself. He found a great sense of inner peace and spiritual concentration within this special room.

Jung kept on adding to the tower throughout his long life. The new bits represented different parts of his ever-evolving psyche. He felt that this was an important part of his own individuation process, as if he was being reborn in stone. Life at Bollingen was kept deliberately simple – there was no electricity, and Jung chopped all his own wood, drew water from a well and cooked all his own food. He enjoyed the sense of silence and living in harmony with nature. All around, he carved inscriptions on stones, expressing different insights. The creative play aspect that Jung enjoyed at Bollingen was very important as a means for him to access and understand his unconscious – a process that many people find difficult.

4

exploring the psyche

Jung emphasized the importance of looking at both the personal unconscious and the collective unconscious when studying the human psyche. Freud saw the unconscious as a kind of dumping ground, where we store unacceptable ideas and thoughts. Jung saw it very differently – for him it was the true basis of the human psyche, 'the innermost mystery of life', from which consciousness arose.

When he talks about the 'psyche', Jung means the whole of the mind or spirit, both conscious and unconscious. The individual psyche is always seeking growth and wholeness and *balance* is of paramount importance. Conscious attitudes are always balanced by unconscious attitudes: if a conscious attitude grows too strong then the unconscious will always seek to restore equilibrium. The unconscious will express its ideas by means of dreams, spontaneous imagery, slips of the tongue and so on. If the unconscious message is ignored, then neurosis or even physical disease may result.

The personal unconscious

Freud's work had made people much more aware of the unconscious and the ways in which it operated in both the adult and the developing child. Freud believed that accessing unconscious, repressed memories was the key to sorting out neuroses. His influence on current thinking had turned the unconscious into a sort of mental rubbish heap, a 'dump for moral refuse'. For Jung, the unconscious was much more than that – it contained *all* aspects of human nature, good and bad. It was no mere rubbish dump, but was infinitely mysterious: not only could it look forward as well as back in time, it could also reach beyond its individual boundaries into the world of the collective unconscious.

Freud was a convinced mechanist and tried always to be strictly scientific in his approach. Jung was also trained in the scientific method and tried to understand the workings of the psyche in terms of biological processes. However, unlike many scientists of his day, Jung never lost his interest in the psychic and paranormal aspects of the human mind. He acknowledged that there was much in life that we cannot yet understand, but this did not mean that one had to pretend it did not exist. In a lecture to the Society for Psychical Research in 1919, he expressed this point of view when he remarked, 'I shall not commit the fashionable stupidity of regarding everything I cannot explain as a fraud.' This difference in attitude was one of several key factors in the rift between Freud and Jung.

In Jung's view the personal unconscious consists mainly of 'complexes'. These are related groups of emotionally charged ideas, thoughts and images. Many complexes may appear in the same person, but they do not have to be negative in effect. They are psychic phenomena that tend to group together because they work more efficiently that way. This is because they tend to be related to a particular archetype. A commonly cited example is the 'mother complex'. There is an inbuilt instinctual ability to recognize the mother's nipple and this is our first experience of 'mother'. Gradually, we add to this all kinds of information about our own mother, and mothers in general, and build up an inner data bank – this is the mother complex. This is constantly expanding and changing as a person matures, so that we may add to it a whole host of other ideas, such as 'mother earth', 'mother nature', 'mother country' and so on. All these relate to the mother archetype and help the psyche to be more organized and efficient.

Complexes can act as a kind of sub-personality, and at times these can manifest themselves as a different character. Such a character may appear in dreams, fantasies or trance states. In cases of mental illness or neurosis, complexes may be in conflict with one another, or their energy may become blocked off. The more negatively charged complexes a person has the more disturbed he or she becomes, because these act as pathological, disrupting factors in the psyche. The immediate goal of analysis of the unconscious is to root out these negative complexes so that their content becomes conscious and the person can stop 'acting out' from them and being ruled by them. The unconscious is always in danger of becoming too one-sided, keeping to well worn paths and getting stuck in dead ends. We are all familiar with the idea of somebody having 'a one-track mind'. Jung stressed that we are never done with working on the unconscious, and should always pay attention to our dreams and fantasies, because they will give us pointers as to where we have become unbalanced.

The collective unconscious

Jung's interest in the collective unconscious began as a result of his work with psychotic patients and his own midlife crisis. He decided that it has two main aspects:

* *archetypes*, which help to give form to our understanding of unconscious ideas;
* *instincts*, which are the innate biological drives that determine our behaviour, e.g. sex drive, hunger, and aggression.

Both these components belong in the collective unconscious because they exist independently of the individual psyche and contain universally recognized, inherited aspects.

Archetypes

Jung says that archetypes are usually religious in their nature, and are accompanied by an atmosphere of the numinous. They are images and have no physical existence in the material world, but this does not mean that they have no separate reality of their own. A good example of an archetype is Jung's spirit guide, Philemon, who is an archetypal sage or wise man. People form different archetypal images according to the culture they live in, but the archetype itself remains the same. Everyone is familiar with archetypal figures that tend to appear in myths and fairy stories, for example, the old woman, the trickster, the youth, the fool and so on.

Instincts

Jung reflected that civilization has forced us to separate from our basic instincts, but they have not disappeared altogether. Because they are often repressed, they tend to show themselves indirectly, for example as a neurosis or as an unaccountable mood. They may also appear in dream images, or manifest as slips of the tongue or memory lapses.

Jung wanted to move away from the idea of separate instincts such as hunger, sex and aggression. He found this approach too concrete and decided that it was more helpful to see the various instincts as being different expressions of a single, motivating psychic energy. He called this energy *libido*, comparing the concept to the one in physics, where heat, light and electricity are all different aspects of physical energy. Freud had used the term libido to describe sexual drive, but Jung stressed that it is important not to select one single motivating instinct in this way, any more than the physicist would say that all forces derive from heat alone.

The ego and the Self

The 'ego' is the centre of consciousness and gives us our sense of who we think we are. It organizes and balances the conscious and unconscious aspects of the psyche, giving it a sense of personal identity and purpose. Jung came to identify his own ego with his analytical (Number 1) personality. The ego is not to be confused with the 'Self', which is the wholeness that the psyche is constantly seeking and moving towards. The Self transcends the ego and is the goal of the individuation process. But a strong ego can exert a balancing influence, keeping the conscious and unconscious aspects of the personality in equilibrium. An over inflated ego, on the other hand, will form a dictatorial, intolerant personality. Such an ego can become highly unpleasant, even dangerous, seeing itself as all-important, almost god-like.

The shadow and projection

The shadow

The 'shadow' is an unconscious part of the personality that contains weaknesses and other aspects of personality that a person cannot admit to having. The ego and the shadow work together as a balancing pair. Jung related the shadow to his intuitive (Number 2) personality. It is usually the first hidden layer of the personality to be encountered when a person begins psychological analysis. One of the primary tasks of the analyst is to begin to make a person aware of the relationship between the ego and the shadow. When a person has a very weak ego they may be in danger of becoming swamped by images from the shadow, rather as Jung himself was during his midlife crisis.

The shadow is the dark side of our nature and often appears in dreams as a dark, usually rather negative figure, who is always the same sex as the dreamer. The ego wishes to hide shadow aspects of the personality, but in fact the shadow is not necessarily 'bad'.

If we face our shadow properly, then it can offer us integration between the conscious and unconscious parts of our psyche.

Projection

The ego often projects the shadow onto other people. Projection is a normal and natural process whereby an unconscious characteristic, a fault, or even a talent of one's own is seen as belonging to another person or object. When the shadow is projected the ego may see the other person or people as being evil and so can conveniently deny any nasty aspects of itself. Projection is always accompanied by a strong emotional reaction to a person, object or situation. Obvious examples are developing a 'crush' on someone, or taking an excessive dislike to someone or something.

Projection is an indication that unconscious ideas are trying to break through into the conscious mind. It is not really the other person or thing that we love or loathe, but a part of our own psyche that is projected onto them. As the psyche matures it is often able to recognize and own its shadow characteristics and the projection is then withdrawn. When we project, we tend to dwell on the attitudes of the other person, and repress criticisms that are trying to surface from our own psyche. These criticisms often appear in dreams.

The Zeitgeist

Jung stresses that the psyche is not confined to the individual. A collective psyche forms the spirit of the age, or 'Zeitgeist'. This collective psyche forms a collective shadow, which can be exceedingly dangerous. For example, in World War II, the Nazis formed a collective shadow which they projected onto the Jewish people, whom they then saw as worthless and evil.

Jung urged mankind to take a good look at itself. He sensed dark, uncontrolled shadow forces building up in civilized society. Society has a tendency to keep its problem aspects tucked away in separate drawers. These deadly, self-created dangers are often projected onto other nations. Jung said that we must recognize that shadow projections are moral problems, which cannot be solved by arms races or economic competition. We need to look at our own shadow, instead of blaming 'them' all the time.

The persona

The 'persona' (from the same Latin word, meaning 'actor's mask') is like a mask that the ego creates in order to hide its true nature from society. It is our public face and may be assumed both deliberately and unconsciously. Whenever we relate to others, we put on this mask. The form of the mask depends on the expectations and conditioning of society, from parents, teachers, peer groups and so on.

It is necessary for each individual to assume a persona sometimes, in order to function normally within society, because it gives some degree of protection to the vulnerable ego. We need it in order to be able to fit in with cultural norms, or to do a particular job. Every profession has its own persona, and it is easy for people to fully identify with their professional image and to hide behind it. This is when problems arise: the person becomes nothing but the role they play. Behaviour becomes rigid, and the person is fearful of dropping the mask. Such a personality becomes confined and liable to develop neuroses. There is a failure to see the broader aspects of life beyond the ego's own tiny role – this situation is spiritually suffocating.

Anima and animus

Jung used the word 'anima' to describe the personification of the unconscious feminine aspect of a man's personality. The 'animus' is the corresponding masculine aspect of a woman's personality. These unconscious aspects of the personality are seen as being very important in regulating behaviour.

The anima

The anima appears in dreams as archetypal figures such as the seductress, harlot or divine female spirit guide. She represents a man's feeling nature, which is fascinating and secretive. Because the anima is composed of feelings, she may distort a man's understanding. She is often associated with earth and water imagery, such as caves, fertile soil, waterfalls or the sea. The anima communicates the images of the unconscious to a man's conscious mind. Jung always questioned his own anima when he felt emotionally disturbed. He found that after a while she would always produce a useful image of some sort and his sense of unrest would vanish. For a man to be in touch with his anima is therefore healing and balancing.

The anima is not a specific woman but an archetype. She contains all the ancestral impressions of what it means to be female. Her form will depend on a man's individual knowledge of women. Passionate attractions occur when the anima is projected onto an actual woman, so that the man falls in love. If, on the other hand, the man over-identifies with the anima, he may become moody, resentful or effeminate. If a man's anima is very weak then he will find relationships with women difficult.

The animus

Jung does not say as much about the corresponding animus in women, probably because he had no direct experience of it in his own psyche. The animus represents the thinking, logical part of the woman's psyche and can lead her towards knowledge and true meaning. It is made up of spontaneous, unpremeditated opinions, which can affect a woman's emotional life. The animus appears in dreams as heroes, poets, gurus and so on. He is also represented in imagery of the air and fire elements, such as swords or burning flames. Projection of the animus onto a real man results in the woman falling in love. The animus likes to project itself onto sporting heroes, intellectuals and so on. If a woman over-identifies with the animus, she becomes dominating, opinionated and pig-headed. The woman's animus development is important in the way she relates to men – if it is weak then she will have problems.

Ideas about the archetypal male or female from myths, dreams and fantasies can lead people to have very distorted ideas about the opposite sex. For example, the little girl who has been raised on 'Sleeping Beauty' type stories might constantly seek a handsome prince. Jung believed that men were naturally polygamous, and that the anima compensated for this by always appearing as a single woman or female image. Women on the other hand were naturally monogamous, so that the animus often appears as whole groups of men. If it functions properly, the anima or animus should act like a sort of bridge or door between the personal unconscious and collective unconscious. In a similar way, the persona acts as a bridge between the ego and the external world.

5

the journey of the psyche

Jung suggested that the psyche worked according to basic scientific principles. We are all born with a built-in human developmental programme, buried deep in the collective unconscious. Our psychic development follows a basic archetypal pattern, much as the physical body grows and develops in accordance with its genetic blueprint. The conscious mind is only part of the picture and it is contained, like a smaller circle, within the larger circle of the unconscious.

The individual psyche is always changing as it seeks growth and wholeness. The archetypal patterns of change, such as birth, marriage and death, are often reflected in special rites of passage. In order to achieve individuation it is important for us always to move forward with the flow of our lives and not get stuck in previous stages of development. The first half of life is about establishing ourselves in the world; later on we become more inward looking and spiritually reflective.

The growth of the psyche

Jung suggested several basic principles at work in the psyche, which he based on scientific principles:

* *The principle of opposites:* everything in the psyche naturally has an opposite aspect – this principle is basic to all of nature.
* *The principle of equivalence:* equal amounts of energy are given to each of the opposites. If we deny the negative aspects they will tend to emerge from the unconscious in dreams, fantasies, slips of tongue and so on.
* *The principle of entropy:* opposite aspects tend eventually to blend together.
* *The principle of homeostasis:* the psyche always seeks to maintain itself in a state of balance.

Jung sees the psyche not as a fixed, static entity, but as constantly changing and developing throughout life. A great deal of the work of personality development goes on at an unconscious level, and throughout life we are influenced by our environment and the people we encounter on our journey.

Jung sees the individuation process as a basic biological process, present in all living organisms, not just in humans. He even saw it occurring in inorganic systems, such as when a crystal forms a definite shape as it grows, suspended in a liquid solution. The goal of individuation is wholeness – a process of each individual organism becoming fully what it was intended to be from the beginning. In other words, for human beings it is a long process of becoming as complete and balanced a human being as we can.

The individuation process is never complete: the spiral path takes us on a lifelong journey. As we travel we gradually unravel the conditioning imposed by our parents and society and peel away what Jung calls the 'false wrappings' of our persona. This frees us to meet our own shadow and acknowledge its power within us, so that we can try to stop projecting it onto others. Gradually, our psyche becomes more balanced and we are able to become much more whole and effective humans.

Archetypal stages of development

The archetypes are the structural elements, or basic patterns, of the collective unconscious: the psychic health of the individual depends on their proper functioning. As it develops, the individual psyche has to go through the same basic stages that occurred in the evolution of consciousness throughout the history of mankind.

Jung explored the archetypal stages mainly through looking at myths and legends. He says that understanding these archetypal stories can help us to understand how the psyche develops, because the individual psyche mirrors the cultural evolution of consciousness that can be traced back through recorded history. The myth of the hero is the most commonly recurring myth throughout the world and it also crops up frequently in people's dreams. It varies enormously in its details, but the underlying theme is always similar: a good example is found in the King Arthur myth. Jung says that the hero story has relevance for the development of individuals as they struggle to establish their own identity. Like the mythical hero, we all encounter a new set of archetypal energies at each stage of our development. We need to integrate these, both in our personality and our behaviour.

Individuation and the Self

Unlike most psychologists of his day, Jung insisted that the development of the psyche extends well beyond childhood and adolescence, even continuing into old age. Jung believed that this process can never become complete unless the individual confronts the monsters that lurk in his own unconscious. He discovered these in his own psyche during his midlife crisis, and they appear throughout myth and legend in archetypal themes such as slaying the dragon.

Taking responsibility for our less favoured aspects (confronting the shadow), is the first task of the Self in the individuation process. Throughout this process the psyche has to continually examine and confront what it produces. The work is not easy, as Jung himself admitted, but it can have great rewards as it helps us to become more peaceful humans, better able to relate effectively to our fellow beings. Once we begin to know the shadow we reach the next layer in the psyche, which is the anima or animus – the opposite-sex image in the psyche. Opposite-sex relationships present us with the stage on which we can explore the interacting anima/animus energies: this explains why they are frequently so difficult! If we are willing to grow together and help one another, we can work towards a mutual understanding.

We can begin to explore the world of the unconscious by means of dreams, because they represent ways in which the unconscious is trying to become conscious. Jung also used active imagination techniques to work further with dream contents and begin to unravel and understand their deeper meaning. These techniques encourage a person to produce fantasy images that are very much like waking dreams and work in much the same way. The important thing is always to seek and retain a sense of balance, connecting with both the inner and outer worlds.

Sex and gender

Psychologists have debated for many years as to whether 'nature' or 'nurture' has the greater effect on our development of gender awareness. Jung said that we are all born with a built-in archetypal pattern that gives us the blueprint for all aspects of psychic development, including our sexuality. He saw masculine and feminine as two major archetypal forces that coexisted as a balancing complementary pair of opposites. As we grow up, we begin to create a persona that reflects the teachings of the society into which we were born. The animus or anima develops to compensate for this, incorporating the characteristics that we are not supposed to show publicly.

At first the child identifies with the mother, which causes a problem for the growing boy, who has to establish a gender identity that is opposite to that of the mother. If all goes well he will be able to transfer his gender identity to his father, or to other masculine figures. This enables him to learn how to function effectively in the outer world. Girls do not have to break away from gender identification with the mother. However, they are expected to develop a strong ego identity and function in the outer world. This means that they too have to follow the hero myth cycle.

Jung says that there is another problem for girls too, because of the ancient archetypal energy that drives the woman towards biological fulfilment by giving birth to and mothering children. In order to do this she has to break the emotional and spiritual bond between herself and her father, because she has to seek a new man to be her mate. Sometimes women resist this archetypal urge, because it drives them away from the world of careers, competition, success and friendship in the outer world. This is one example of the problems that Jung suggested our modern psyches will encounter when they try to develop along lines that have been laid down by thousands of years of evolution. He warns that our personal psychology is only skin deep, like a ripple on the ocean of the collective unconscious. Collective psychology is the most powerful force in our lives, the one that changes the world and makes history.

Rites of passage

Throughout life we all pass through different stages which bring change into our lives. Many of these changes are marked by special ceremonies. One of the most important ancient rituals is the initiation rite to mark puberty. Jung says that all primitive groups and tribes that are at all organized have special rites of initiation to mark puberty. These are very important in the social and religious life of the tribe. For both sexes the chief aim of these rites of puberty is to separate the young person from the parents, and mark a definite end to childhood.

In the childish stage of consciousness there are usually few problems for the psyche, because everything is taken care of by the parents. For Jung, puberty marks psychic birth, bringing with it a conscious distinction of the ego from the parents – the birth of the hero. From then onwards the demands of life put an end to the dreams of childhood and, if all goes well, the person will be able to make the transition to adulthood and independence. For others, this stage is not easy and they soon run into problems, usually connected with sexual issues or a sense of inferiority. Unfortunately, in the modern world initiation rites have either vanished or turned into shadowy imitations, so that many people do not get any help in reaching maturity. Jung says that because of the archetypal roots deep in our psyche, we still need and crave ritual.

Midlife crisis

As we approach middle age it often seems that we have got everything sorted out at last. Hopefully by now we have established our personal views and social positions, our careers and so on. But many people get stuck at this point. We have to concentrate on certain aspects of interest and push others away: there simply is not time or scope to do everything we would like to do!

Suddenly at the mid-point of our lives it dawns on us that time is beginning to run out. This is the time of the midlife crisis, which Jung says is frequently marked by a period of depression. Once again, a significant change is being prepared for in the human psyche. It may appear as a slow change in a person's personality or interests, or certain traits from childhood may re-emerge. This marks an attempt on the part of the psyche to re-balance itself. Jung says that this stage is very important, because otherwise we risk developing the kind of personality that attempts always to recreate the psychic disposition of youth. Such a personality becomes wooden, boring and stereotyped.

Ageing

Jung says that the second half of life should have a very different quality from the first half. He compares the journey of the psyche to the daily journey of the sun, rising towards the zenith and then falling again. In the first half of life we are concerned with achievement, establishing ourselves in the world, earning a living, raising a family and so on. The problems we encounter are mainly biological and social. Later in life we can hopefully afford to become more inward looking and reflective. The problems we are involved with become more cultural and spiritual in nature. Confronting and integrating the repressed aspects of the personality may lead eventually to the individuation of the psyche.

Jung warns that we cannot live the afternoon of life as we did the morning: what was great in the morning will be seen to be little in the evening, and what was true in the morning will become a lie. At this stage it is essential to begin to explore the world within the psyche if we wish to stay psychologically healthy: we must begin to understand ourselves and our spiritual nature. But this is not always easy, and many people prefer to get stuck in the past, perhaps becoming endlessly moaning victims, tedious eternal adolescents or stuffy, boring old doctrinaires.

With old age the psyche reaches the final stage in its cyclical journey. The first stage was childhood, where we were a problem to others, but not yet conscious of self-responsibility. Next came youth and middle age, with its conscious problems. The final stage is extreme old age, when we often once again become a problem for others. Although childhood and old age are very different stages, they have in common a submersion in the world of the unconscious, into which we must all ultimately vanish.

6

dreams and symbols

Dreams were very important to Jung and took a central place in analytical psychology. He suggested various different functions that dreams serve and said that they can arise from many different sources. He said that he had no fixed dream theory: each dream has a meaning that is relevant to the individual, and thus it can help with the individuation process.

Interpretation should always be carried out by means of talking to the dreamer about the dream itself. Dreams can reflect many different aspects of the life of an individual and dream symbols may have relevance to society as a whole, as well as to the individual. Therefore, the analyst needs to have a good grasp of mythological ideas so that dreams can be looked at in a collective context. It is often helpful to look at a whole series of dreams that have a connecting theme, because this will lead to fresh insights.

The importance of dreams

For Jung, dreams, archetypes and other mental imagery had a separate psychic reality of their own. He suggested various different functions that dreams serve:

* to act as compensation for areas of the conscious mind that are deficient or distorted in some way;
* to bring back archetypal memories from the collective unconscious;
* to draw attention to both inner and outer aspects of our lives of which we are not consciously aware.

Freud saw dreams as important starting points for triggering off the free association process. He would pick out a particular symbol and see where the associated train of thought led. Jung felt that this approach was rather limited for several reasons:

* it debases the rich symbolism and imagery contained in many dreams;
* it often leads one off on another path entirely, away from the original meaning of the dream;
* the dream expresses something that the unconscious is trying to convey – therefore, it is more important to look at the content of the dream.

Jung agreed with Freud when he said that dreams often arise from emotional upsets, in which complexes are also frequently involved. These complexes are like tender spots in the psyche that easily react to external stimulus or disturbance. However, Jung pointed out that complexes can also be explored by means of word association tests, meditation, or conversation – they do not have to wait to be uncovered by a dream.

Jung felt that a dream always had an underlying idea or intention – it is expressing something important that the unconscious wants to say. The intention of the dream can act as a key to helping a person with their individuation process. This is why Jung felt it was important to concentrate on the content of the dream, rather than spinning off on a tangent. Once again, Jung is urging that we listen to what the individual patient or dream has to say. To know and understand a person's whole personality and psychic reality, it is vital to realize that dreams and symbolic imagery have a very important role to play. Jung saw this insight as a turning point in his psychology.

Jung also began to understand that just as the human embryo develops through the stages of its evolutionary history, so the mind also travels on its own evolutionary journey. Dreams allow recall of past memories, right back into childhood and beyond, to the most primitive instincts from the collective unconscious. As Freud had already recognized, such recall can be very healing in some cases, filling in gaps in memory from infancy and bringing balance or enrichment to the adult psyche. The further a person goes into analysis, the more complex and symbolic their dreams tend to get. They begin to extend beyond personal life and its experiences, into the realm of the collective and mythological.

Symbols

Jung was particularly interested in the symbolism that appeared in dreams. The strange mythological fragments that appeared in his own dreams and fantasies and those of his patients were rich in archetypal symbolism. He found that they were often highly numinous in character and therefore felt that they were very important for the growth of the psyche.

A symbol is a term, a name or an image that contains special associations in addition to its obvious everyday meaning. For example, a rainbow can be a symbol for joy and hope of good things to come. A symbol differs from a sign in that a sign is always *less* than the concept that it represents, whereas a symbol stands for something *more* than its obvious meaning. Symbols often occur spontaneously in dreams and also crop up as symbolic thoughts, acts and even situations. Dreams are not invented consciously – they occur spontaneously and are our main source of knowledge about symbolism. Sometimes inanimate objects are involved in symbolic events; for example, the clock that symbolically stops when someone dies.

Many symbols are not just meaningful for the individual, but are collective. These are often religious symbols, such as the ox, lion, man and eagle that represent the four evangelists in the Christian religion. Animals very often crop up as religious symbols. In Egyptian mythology, for example, the gods are represented as having attributes of animals such as the jackal, hawk and cat. This type of symbolism is used to express ideas that are beyond words. The origin of typical religious symbols is often attributed to the gods themselves but Jung says that they arise from spontaneous primeval dreams and fantasies.

A good deal of our perception of reality goes on at a subconscious level, because we are so bombarded with stimuli all the time that we could not possibly register them all. We perceive many more events than are registered consciously. Sometimes these events well up from the subconscious later on – perhaps in a moment of intuition or in a dream. We then realize that they hold emotional meaning or other significance. Jung says that dream symbols are mostly manifestations of the area of the psyche that lies beyond the control of the conscious mind. He likens the way in which the psyche spontaneously produces symbols to the way in which a plant produces a flower. Dreams are therefore seen as evidence of psychic activity and growth.

The origins of dreams

There can be many different causes for dreams and Jung discusses different aspects of the question of their origin.

* *Physical causes:* such as having eaten a huge meal before going to bed.

* *Memory recall:* this may be from the distant past, or just mulling over events from the previous day.
* *Compensations:* for things that one lacks in waking life. Such a dream may highlight a hidden wish or conflict. Recurring dreams are often attempts to compensate for particular defects in a person's attitude to life. Such conflicts may date from childhood.
* *Looking ahead:* this includes warning dreams and those where we worry about forthcoming events, as well as the more mysterious precognitive dream. Crises in our lives often have a long unconscious history before they happen. Recurring dreams may also fall into this category.
* *Oracular dreams:* these are dreams that feel numinous and highly significant to the dreamer – the sort of dream that our ancestors would have interpreted as messages from the gods. They are sometimes precognitive.

Archetypes in dreams

Archetypal images and figures that appear in dreams are not the archetype itself – they are simply representations of it. For example, a dream of the Virgin Mary could represent the divine mother archetype. Jung explains that archetypes are closely connected to instincts. Instincts, he says, are physiological urges, which can be perceived by the normal senses, but can also manifest as symbolic images – these are the archetypes.

Archetypes sometimes appear in children's dreams, like Jung's own phallus dream. In *Man and his Symbols*, he gives an example of a whole series of dreams recorded and drawn by a ten-year-old girl. The archetypal content is very strong, including an evil, snake-like monster that comes and eats all the other animals, and a drunken woman who falls into water and emerges renewed and sober. So far as Jung was able to discover, these images were not related to any mythological ideas or religious beliefs that her family held.

Analysing dreams

For Jung, the dream story was not like a conscious story, with a logical beginning, middle and end. It was a complex intuitive structure, which must be viewed as a whole, rather than by being picked apart. He also felt that it was important to look at the imagery in the individual dream. Each image needs to be considered in turn, always looking at it within the context of the dreamer's own life. For example, suppose someone dreams that they are using a stick to beat down a door. For Freud, this would be an obvious sexual symbol, with the stick representing a phallus. But Jung pointed out that it could mean something else entirely. The unconscious has deliberately chosen this particular symbol – the analyst's task is to find out why.

Even common dream themes such as falling, flying and so on must be viewed in terms of the dream itself. Each dream arises from the individual psyche, in answer to specific circumstances and emotions. It is therefore not possible to lay down general rules for dream interpretation and we should be careful never to impose a meaning on somebody else's dream. We can never fully understand another person's dream and so it is vital to keep our own flow of associations in check. In Jungian analysis:

* the dream should always be treated as a fact – we should make no previous assumptions about it;
* the dream is a specific creation from the unconscious that somehow makes sense, even if we cannot immediately see how;
* we should explore the content of the dream thoroughly to try and find out what unconscious message is trying to emerge.

Dreams have a tendency to occur in series, each separate dream conveying an underlying message in a slightly different way.

Jung found that, as a rule, a series of dreams was more useful for interpretation than a single dream. This is because important points become clearer with repetition, and mistakes in interpretation are often corrected by analysing a subsequent dream. The dream can be approached in various different ways.

* *Objectively:* the dream is considered in terms of the person's real life in the external world. For example, if you dream that your car has broken down, perhaps the dream is telling you that it is time to take your car in for a service.

* *Subjectively:* the dream is considered in terms of what it represents within the person's own personality. This time the car might represent yourself – perhaps there is a hidden health problem nagging away at your unconscious mind.

* *Collectively:* if the dream contains numinous, archetypal symbols then we can look towards the collective unconscious and mythological interpretations. For example, if a woman dreams about a brave young warrior, this could be her animus bringing her a message about her need to be more assertive.

Jung's house dream

Jung gives an example of a dream that he had about a house and uses it to describe some of the possible pitfalls of interpreting another person's dream. In this dream he was exploring a house on various different levels. He began on the first floor, which was furnished in the style of the eighteenth century. Below this, the ground floor was dark and appeared to be furnished more in sixteenth century style. The lower down he went, the more primitive the house became, and the cellar was Roman. In the floor of the cellar was a stone slab, which revealed the way down to a cave full of prehistoric bones and skulls.

When Jung analysed this dream he realized that it was a sort of summary of his own life. He grew up in a house that was about 200 years old, and his parents' attitude was in many ways medieval. The lower levels illustrated his passionate interest in ancient history and palaeontology. However, when Jung discussed this dream with Freud, Freud became obsessed with the image of the bones and skulls. He kept returning to them over and over again, insisting that Jung try to find a wish in connection with them. Jung soon realized that Freud was hinting at a hidden death wish, directed at Freud himself!

Jung realized that this was his dream, about his own private world. This was important because he came to understand that dream analysis is not a technique that can be learned and applied by following strict rules – it has to be done by means of discussion between two people. The danger is always that the analyst's interpretation might dominate that of the client. Jung gave up using hypnosis for the same reason.

Sometimes a dream or vision cannot be understood however much one tries to investigate it. Jung says that in this case it is best then to leave it at the back of the mind, because it may become clearer at a later date. Often an external event will clarify a dream that one has long been mulling over. Jung says that if one carries a dream around for long enough some sense will always emerge from it.

For Jung, dreams and symbols are never pointless or meaningless. They are often not directly connected with worldly concerns, which is why many people tend to dismiss them as being unimportant. Jung says that to him it is incredible that although we get messages from our unconscious psyche almost every night, most people cannot be bothered to explore their meaning and often even mistrust or despise them. He wonders what the unconscious thinks of us! Jung was never able to agree with Freud that a dream was merely a façade, behind which lurked a meaning that was already known but was being withheld from consciousness. Dreams, for Jung, are often difficult to understand because they are expressed in symbols and pictures, which form the language of the unconscious. They are not deliberately deceptive – they are simply natural attempts by the unconscious to express ideas in its own way.

7

the
personality
and
relationships

Jung observed that human behaviour tends to follow certain basic patterns, which often operate as pairs of opposites. During the course of development, one of each pair often comes to be preferred so that the person tends to develop that mode of behaviour and act according to its characteristic aspects. The preferred mode of behaviour gradually becomes habitual and leads to predictable personality traits and ways of behaving.

He identified two opposite and balanced 'attitudes' in human personalities. These were 'introversion', where psychic energy is turned inwards, towards the inner world and 'extroversion', where psychic energy is turned outwards, towards the external world. He then established four different 'functions', which he called 'thinking', 'feeling', 'sensation' and 'intuition'. A person's conscious orientation will usually be towards one principal function, which will determine how the person reacts to experiences. Jung then combined the two attitudes and the four functions to produce eight different psychological 'types'.

Introversion and extroversion

Jung's theory divided people into two basic types according to the orientation of their psychic energy. The two different attitudes were called 'introversion' and 'extroversion', and the two psychological types 'introverts' and 'extroverts'. These terms are so well known today that people take them for granted in everyday use. Everyone has both attitudes to varying degrees, but there is a tendency for one of them to dominate.

* *Introverts* withdraw energy from the world and are more interested in their own inner world than the external world. They are reflective, hesitant people, with retiring natures, preferring to keep themselves to themselves. They often shrink away from new objects and situations and may appear to be somewhat defensive. Introverts need privacy and personal space.

* *Extroverts* direct their energy outwards towards the world and are more interested in external things and relationships. They are outgoing and frank, with accommodating, adaptable personalities. Extroverts need action and other people around them.

Usually one or other attitude will dominate in the personality and the opposite attitude becomes unconscious. The psyche will then tend to find compensatory ways of expressing this hidden attitude. The two types of attitude tend to clash because where the extrovert will follow the crowd, the introvert will deliberately reject the majority view. The introvert likes peace and solitude, whereas the extrovert likes to be active and sociable.

Jung realized that nobody ever fitted exactly into one type. People have an infinite variety of different personalities and it would be too narrow and simplistic to fit them neatly into two categories. Because we all possess both attitudes, it is more a question of whether one predominates over the other. Jung's theory is not really attempting to explain *individual* psychology – it is a generalization, aimed at trying to explain human behaviour.

He developed his theory about personality to include four 'functions' in addition to the two attitudes.

The four functions

The idea of there being four balanced elements within nature is very old. Shamanic and magical traditions often use a system where four elements – earth, air, fire and water – are related to four directions – north, east, south and west. Each element is also associated with different corresponding energies that are represented symbolically by animals, plants, seasons, colours and so on. For example, south is usually associated with the fire element, so an appropriate animal might be a dragon, the colour could be red and the season summer.

Long ago in Ancient Greece, doctors and philosophers began to identify four personality types, based on the same idea of four balanced natural energies. These types, or 'humours', were: melancholic, sanguine, choleric and phlegmatic. Jung developed a theory of four personality functions based on a similar idea. His 'four functions' are grouped as two opposite pairs, giving them a feeling of balance. He named the four functions: *thinking*, *feeling*, *sensation* and *intuition*.

Thinking and feeling are classed as 'rational' functions, because they rely on internal mental processes. They determine the way in which a person judges and evaluates experiences. Sensation and intuition are classed as 'irrational' functions because they rely on objective stimuli. They determine the way in which a person perceives experiences.

A person's conscious orientation will usually be towards one of the four functions. This dominant function will determine how the person reacts to experiences. Its opposite function remains largely unconscious and the two left over functions are partially conscious, partially unconscious. When the conscious function is particularly strong, there is a tendency for the opposite function to break through into consciousness now and again. This is called 'the return of the repressed' and it may manifest as hysteria, phobias, obsessions, unbalanced moods and so on. In order to gain a balanced, healthy mental attitude it is often necessary to work with the repressed function in therapy.

Thinking

This tells you what something is. Thinking people have logical, probing and questioning minds. They are good at seeing cause and effect, judging things and reaching logical conclusions by using their intellect. They are frank and may appear cool and distant emotionally. This kind of person is good at adapting to new circumstances.

Feeling

This tells you whether something is agreeable to you or not. Feeling people make judgements about how they value things. Jung stresses that 'feeling' is not used here in the emotional sense – that would imply irrational thinking. Jung is referring here to a rational function, used for putting things in order of value. Feeling people have a strong sense of traditional values and human relationships are important to them. They are often warm, creative people.

Sensation

This tells you that something exists. This kind of person relies very much on sensory impressions. They assess their world by how things look, what words sound like and so on. Material things are very important to them and they are solid, grounded people. They take everything at face value and 'call a spade a spade'. They can be boring and plodding, lacking in imagination, but on the other hand they are often jolly and easy-going. Their calm nature makes them appear rational and logical, but this is not always the case.

Intuition

This gives you hunches about things. This kind of person is aware of chances, possibilities, the past and the future. They are often not aware of their own bodies and may be dreamy and ungrounded. They can become impatient with solid, monotonous detail and they are not practical people. Intuitive people are able to perceive possibilities that are not known consciously through the normal senses.

The eight psychological types

Each of the four functional kinds of personality may be extroverted or introverted. Jung therefore combined the four functions and the two attitudes, to arrive at eight 'psychological types'. A person's psychological type is important in determining their view of the world and how they cope with situations and relationships.

Extrovert thinking

This type is dominated by rational thinking and logic. They love order and facts, and tend to think that their view of the world is the correct one. In fact they conveniently suppress anything that doesn't fit in with their world view and they have a tendency to become tyrants. What they repress may return as violent moods, wild love affairs and so on. They have a strong sense of duty, but they may lack warmth and tolerance. Many scientists and engineers may belong to this type.

Introvert thinking

This type is more interested in the inner world of ideas than external facts. They constantly ask questions and formulate theories about things, but they are reserved about accepting 'facts'. They may appear eccentric to others and may be so cut off from the world that relationships are unimportant to them. Philosophers and other academics may belong to this type.

Extrovert feeling

This type is well-adjusted to the world around, and fits in well with the peer group. They are conventional, concerned with personal success. They are tactful and charming, handling people well, and enjoy social gatherings and groups. On the negative side, they can be rather shallow and insincere. Event organizers and public relations people may belong to this group.

Introvert feeling

This type is rather remote and inward looking – the 'still waters run deep' type of person. They are reserved and enjoy peace and quiet, poetry and music. They prefer to have a few intimate friends and understand people close to them pretty well. They are often very religious and self-sacrificing. These people are usually very genuine because they are hopeless at role-playing, and they make loyal friends. Monks and nuns may belong to this group.

Extrovert sensation

For this type, objects and sensations in the outside world are very important. This is the practical, man-of-the-world type who accepts the world as it is and enjoys living in it. The down side is that they can be addictive and pleasure seeking and sometimes have a tendency towards perversion. People of this type are often in business or property dealing.

Introvert sensation

With this type. the internal, subjectively experienced sensation is important. Objects do not count much to this type. They are so full of their own sensations that they may appear out of touch and find it hard to express themselves to others. They may claim to see ghosts, visions and startling imagery. Some artists and musicians may belong to this group.

Extrovert intuitive

This type uses the intuitive part of the brain whenever a judgement or decision has to be made without knowing the full facts. They get bored with fixed, familiar, well-established things and like to explore the new and look to the future. Because of this they may view customs and convention as unimportant and may trample on other people in order to get what they want. They are 'chancers', with their own form of morality. They rarely see a thing through to the end, and their personal relationships are weak. Entrepreneurs and businessmen may belong to this group.

Introvert intuitive

To this type, the mystical world of dreams, visions and the collective unconscious is important. They are often pre-occupied with inner daydreams, fantasies and religious revelations. In the past this type of person would have probably been the shaman of the tribe, but nowadays they are often rather outcast and regarded as being 'odd'. Many psychics, mystics and poets belong in this group.

Forming relationships

Gaining insight into a person's psychological type can assist progress in therapy or help to understand a relationship. People may gradually change their type as they develop and mature. Integration of the different types within the personality can be seen as the goal of the individuation process. The more mature the psyche becomes, the more a person is consciously aware of different aspects of the self. It is rare, if not impossible, to find a person who represents a pure type. The types are really intended to represent general behavioural tendencies, rather than concrete personality categories. Most people are a mixture of at least two types and more complex personalities probably incorporate more.

People are often attracted to their opposite type because their partner expresses the neglected function. There are two dangers here.

* People may avoid achieving their own psychological wholeness because they see their neglected function as belonging to the other person.
* Because opposite types do not understand each other, many misunderstandings can arise.

When a person projects their own hidden aspect onto someone else they 'fall in love' with them. As they become more aware of their own unconscious aspect this projection tends to be withdrawn and they fall out of love again.

Sometimes people fall for the same type as themselves. This means that the dominant function tends to get over emphasized and the suppressed one causes all sorts of havoc in the relationship. For example, two introverted, intuitive poets might get together and live in a little fantasy world, totally neglecting their surroundings and living in squalor.

The developing psyche

A person's psychological type begins to become apparent quite early in childhood. It is determined by a number of different factors:

* *Heredity:* genetic factors will tend to predispose a child to being more introverted or extroverted.
* *Parental type:* the child may identify with one or other parent and so begin to copy their behaviour. Alternatively they may deliberately develop an opposite type in order to rebel.
* *Social factors:* whichever behaviour is encouraged and achieves the best results will also influence the development of a psychological type. The family, school, peer group and so on are all important here. Extrovert children soon appear to be more active, talkative, sociable and interested in their surroundings. This type of outlook is favoured in modern Western society and so will tend to be encouraged.

Problems often arise when parents try to force a child into a mould that goes against the natural type. This sort of pressure can result in neurosis and hampers development in later life. If the parents are more flexible they can help the child towards individuation. Often the unconscious function is projected onto others as the child grows – perhaps onto parents, siblings, peer group members, actors or pop stars. The child will identify with groups or fall in love with people who satisfy this function. Through a process of repeated projection and subsequent withdrawal, the psyche gradually becomes more integrated. This is why attachments of this sort are so important to the developing psyche.

the esoteric and the paranormal

'Esoteric' knowledge is secret or mystical knowledge, revealed only to those 'in the know'; 'paranormal' refers to things that cannot be explained by objective methods within the framework of current understanding. Jung covered a wide range of esoteric and paranormal studies in his search for universal truths within human psychology that would link up with his theories about the collective unconscious.

Jung studied Gnosticism (a religious and philosophical movement), astrology, alchemy and the I Ching (a method of divination) in order to explore aspects of mysticism, magic, science and religion. In these studies he discovered much archetypal symbolism and mythology that supported his theories. He was also interested in coincidences, believing that events in the outer world of material things were often reflected in the inner world of the psyche and vice versa. This is a view that is currently supported by theories in quantum physics.

Gnosticism

Gnosticism was a religious and philosophical movement, which probably originated in around the fourth century BCE. There were many different Gnostic sects, all concerned with knowledge of the occult and the magical. *Gnosis* is derived from a Greek word, meaning 'knowledge'.

Jung studied Gnosticism in depth from about 1918 until 1926. His interest first arose because he was keen to establish historical and literary links with his ideas about human psychology. He saw his analytical psychology as being fundamentally a natural science but he was well aware that, because of the nature of the beast, it was easy to introduce personal bias to his findings. He needed some kind of credibility and he thought that this might be achieved if he could demonstrate parallels between his own thinking and that of the Gnostics.

Jung discovered that mythological ideas within Gnosticism had great relevance to his ideas about the human psyche. In Gnostic thinking nature and creation are fundamentally flawed and separated from the original true God. The world is ruled over by its creator, who is not really the original god, but a sort of 'half-god' or 'demi-urge'. He is assisted by seven beings called 'archons', who try to enslave people and prevent their return to the original divine realm. Gnosis was supposed to offer a key to the return to the divine.

Jung saw this myth as being symbolic of the individuation process, where the soul goes on its own inner spiritual quest, seeking inner unity with the Self. At the start of the quest, it is as blind to its true nature as the Gnostic soul is to the nature of the true god. Jung was excited about this because it seemed to show that his ideas were not new. Eventually, however, he decided that Gnostic teachings were too remote and obscure – they had been formulated a very long time ago, and any knowledge of them was mainly recorded by Christians, who were rivals to the Gnostics.

Alchemy

Alchemy was very popular during medieval times, but its roots stretch back much further. The best known aspect of alchemy is the idea of trying to turn base metals into gold, but there was a lot more to it than that. The ultimate goal was an inner transformation of the alchemist's psyche, and it was this aspect that interested Jung the most. He saw alchemy as bridging the frustrating gap between ancient Gnosticism and modern sciences, such as chemistry, and the psychology of the unconscious. Alchemical thought coincided in surprising ways with his own ideas about the unconscious, so Jung saw alchemy as the historical counterpart of his analytical psychology that he had been looking for. This gave more substance to his ideas.

Alchemy is full of fantasy images, which Jung soon realized were archetypal in nature. This was important because he realized that understanding historical ideas could be vital in understanding the psychology of the unconscious. The idea of turning base metal into gold was rooted in still earlier ideas about the four elements – earth, air, fire and water. Every physical form was supposed to contain these four elements in different proportions. If one could somehow alter the balance, then bingo – base metal into gold! Success depended very much on the alchemist's state of mind, which naturally had to be pure, so prayer and meditation were part of the practice.

Jung was intrigued to find alchemical imagery cropping up in the dreams of patients who were going through the individuation process. He studied the alchemical process and found that it went through a series of stages, each one of which could also represent a stage in the development of the maturing psyche.

* *Nigredo* ('blackness') corresponds to the start of analysis, when a person begins to break down the barriers between conscious and unconscious. This stage is often accompanied by depression, as the person begins to face the inner darkness of the shadow.

* *Albedo* ('whiteness') corresponds to the gradual cleansing of the psyche. People often confront and converse with archetypes at this stage, and interestingly the alchemists reported meeting all kinds of frightening archetypal beings wondering around their labs.
* *Rubedo* ('redness') is the final stage, corresponding to resolution of psychic conflicts and the balancing of opposites. Jung remarked that much of his work was concerned with this type of balancing process.

The I Ching

Jung developed a special interest in the I Ching, an ancient Chinese method of divination. From ancient times the Chinese have seen creation as being made up of intertwined male and female energies, each carrying the seed of the other. This is represented by the well-known black and white yin and yang symbol.

The universe is in a constant state of change as the two primal forces flow in and out of each other. This idea of wholeness and the balancing of two opposite forces fit in very well with Jung's ideas, and the yin and yang symbol is another example of the archetypal mandala. To consult the I Ching, yarrow stalks or coins were usually used. Short and long stalks, or the two sides of a coin, represented the two primal forces. The stalks or coins were thrown and the random patterns they made interpreted by using a special book of wise sayings. Jung, in the peace of his retreat at Bollingen, used reeds in place of yarrow stalks.

Jung was fascinated by the results he obtained from I Ching readings. He found many meaningful connections with his own thought processes which he could not explain to himself. He began to use the I Ching with his patients too, and found that a significant number of the answers given were relevant to the patients' problems. For example a young client was wondering whether he should marry a certain girl. When the I Ching was consulted it gave the reply: 'the maiden is powerful. One should not marry such a maiden.' The girl seemed suitable, but deep down the young man was afraid that she would soon become like his dominating mother.

Jung began to wonder how such meaningful answers could emerge from the I Ching. How did the connection between the inner, psychic event and the outer, physical event come about? Jung suggested the idea of 'acausal parallelism', by which he meant that two events could be connected in some way, without one necessarily having to be the direct cause of the other. He later used the word 'synchronicity' to express this idea.

Synchronicity

Science has tended to train people to think that A causes B which causes C, in a neat orderly, linear fashion. So related events are connected by cause and effect – this idea is known as 'causality'. Jung wondered if a 'law of synchronicity' could be established, contrasting with the 'law of causality'. He was very excited by the idea of discovering a place where psychology and physics could meet and some scientists, notably Nobel Prize winner Wolfgang Pauli (1945, Nobel Laureate in Physics), were interested in Jung's ideas. Modern quantum physics seems happy to accept acausal effects in its physical theories. Physicists have even suggested that physical bodies can sometimes have an effect on one another without any apparent exchange of energy taking place between them. The universe seems to consist no longer of facts, but of possibilities.

Jung was especially interested in the more startling coincidences, those that seemed to be so meaningful that it was virtually impossible for them to have occurred by chance alone. Simple coincidences, such as reading a new word in the paper and then immediately coming across it in the crossword, did not hold quite such fascination for him.

For example, he was listening one day to a young woman patient who was relating to him a dream about being given a golden scarab. As she spoke he heard a tapping on the window, and on opening it he found a scarabaeid beetle, the local equivalent of the golden scarab. The woman was so surprised by this event that it changed her whole way of thinking, breaking down her rational defences and leading to new mental maturity. The scarab, as Jung pointed out, is an archetypal symbol of rebirth. Such archetypal symbolism often seems to crop up in connection with synchronous events.

Astrology

Jung was interested in astrology because it also tied up with his ideas about archetypes and the collective unconscious. He did a great deal of careful research, learning how to draw up natal charts and finding out how they linked up with events in people's lives. He was fascinated by the idea that a person's private world could be affected by far-reaching aspects of cosmic activity. He was not at all interested in the generalized astrology that appears in newspapers and magazines.

Jung decided that astrology would be a good way of doing experiments to show synchronicity at work as a natural law in its own right. He studied the birth charts of married couples to see if the positions of the planets in the two natal charts tied in with the marriage event. If this could be shown to happen then he would have established a meaningful acausal link. He did not find a direct correlation but what he did find was equally fascinating. He found that the results of analysis varied according to who was doing the analysis. In other words, a person's subjective expectations were somehow mirrored in the results. Modern physics is beginning to see this as a real possibility – the observer can affect the results of an experiment simply by the act of observing.

As above so below

Jung's view of the human psyche in many ways reflected the ancient occult maxim 'as above so below'. For him events in the outer world of material things were often reflected in the inner world of the psyche. This effect could also take place in reverse, with the individual affecting the surroundings. Jung discovered that as patients got deeper into therapy, synchronous psychic events became more frequent in their lives. He concluded that a human being is not an isolated psyche, but part of a vast network of interacting energy that can affect us in many unexpected ways. Since psyche and matter are part of the same unfathomable universe, and are in constant contact with each other, Jung thought it possible that they represented two different aspects of a whole. As in so many ways, his thinking here was way ahead of his time.

Jung felt that a lot of personal psychological problems arose from a sort of family or cultural karma – problems that had not been resolved by one's forebears were passed on to be sorted out. He said that many problems are more to do with the social environment than the individual and are therefore linked to the collective unconscious. Jung observed that so far psychological therapy had been slow to take this into account.

Jung's view of the world was often subjective, concentrating on the inner world of dreams, visions and synchronous events. He saw his life's quest as being one of achieving understanding of his own unconscious, and so in many ways the inner world was even more important than the outer world. At times he would deliberately try to shut himself off from the sensory input of the outside world and spend time alone in order to enter his own rich inner world. He said that it is essential to listen to the voice of the unconscious in order to balance the historical psychological aspects of our psyche with the ever-changing conditions of the present.

Through his esoteric studies, in the peace and silence of his retreat at Bollingen, Jung was able to achieve this state of being and 'see life in the round'. His huge diversity of interests has caused varying reactions to his work – some have seen him as a genius and a great guru, whereas others have slated him as a charlatan, mainly because of his interest in secret knowledge, the mysterious and the paranormal.

9

religion and spirituality

Jung saw the spiritual aspects of human experience as being of vital importance to the health of the psyche, emphasizing the importance of individual experience. He found the more dogmatic, fundamentalist religions unhelpful because they lead to disagreement and spiritual stagnation. He believed that religions need to grow and evolve in order to answer our deep spiritual needs.

All his life Jung grappled with the problem of evil, which he explored in two books, *Aion* and *Answer to Job*. He studied a wide range of different religions, particularly Buddhism and Hinduism, in order to gain insight into archetypal patterns in religious thinking. He decided that Eastern religions were mainly introverted, looking for meaning within the Self. Western religions on the other hand were more extroverted, searching for meaning in the 'real world'. Jung pointed out that truth lay both without and within, so that neither point of view was completely right nor completely wrong.

The problem of evil

Jung found the conservative dogma and ritual of his father's type of Christianity too limiting. He emphasized that for him the Christian insistence that God the Father and his son Jesus were sinless beings represented an unbalanced attitude – a total denial of the shadow. He predicted an inevitable swing to counteract this trend, which he saw beginning with the nineteenth century teachings of thinkers, such as Marx and Darwin, whose rationalist, materialist stance came into conflict with Christianity. But Jung felt that modern man had gained scientific insight at the cost of losing his soul – he was no longer in contact with the numinous.

Jung asserted that none of us is without our darker aspects. A lack of understanding of what goes on in the unconscious is dangerous because it means that we are afraid to confront the shadow and therefore do not develop the capacity to deal with evil. Jung's attitude to the problem of evil is probably the most important way in which his thinking differs from traditional Christian theology. For Jung, in fact, God was both 'the annihilating fire and an indescribable grace'. Once again we find balanced opposites, which are so important in Jung's thinking.

The story of Job

One of Jung's most controversial books was *Answer to Job*, published near the end of his life in 1952. Jung uses his own interpretation of the Old Testament story of Job to explore his idea of the shadow aspect of God. The story tells of how the devil bets God that Job will turn against him if he is tormented enough. God takes up the devil's bet, and sends Job all kinds of nasty trials and tribulations. Jung's fundamental question is: if God is all-good, then where does evil come from, and how does God permit it to exist? Jung suggests that the Old Testament God, who torments Job, is unpleasant and frightening and yet he demands love from Job. For Jung this is a demonstration of God's shadow side.

Jung's idea is that God goes through an individuation process of his own, gradually becoming more mature and whole. He traces the course of this development through the Bible until we reach the point where God wants to transform himself through becoming human. Eventually, by being incarnated as Jesus, God fully experiences what he had made Job suffer.

The notion that God could have a negative, shadow side has perturbed many Christians. But Jung's idea is that we all need to transform the negativity in ourselves before we can hope to transform the outer world. This is what we are trying to do in the search for the Self. The Self represents a deeper, wiser aspect of our being that knows our life's purpose and our true path.

The journey towards the Self

Jung saw Christ as providing people with an archetypal image of the Self, to which they can aspire. Other religions also have their own figure, such as Buddha, who represents spiritual perfection and wholeness. Just as God sent his son Christ into the world, so each of us sends our ego into the outer world on a quest for individuation, whereon the ego ceases to occupy centre stage in our consciousness. This is a lengthy and very painful process, which Jung compares with the difficult initiation tests often undergone by members of shamanic tribes. Such tests are often designed to bring initiates to the brink of death, after which they emerge with new spiritual awareness. After this the shaman is able to be a healer and spiritual teacher.

Jung identifies this archetypal death and rebirth process occurring in different forms in many cultures and religious traditions, for example in:

* the death and resurrection of Jesus;
* the alchemical process where a base metal is broken down and eventually transmuted into the *Elixir Vitae*;
* shamanic initiation rituals;
* ancient Egyptian myths, where again the god dies and is re-born.

Interestingly, in the Egyptian tradition rebirth was originally only for the Pharaoh, who was a God-like being, but eventually it was available to others who followed the correct burial rites. Jung's vision was that eventually a kind of psychic rebirth would be available for anyone willing to undergo the individuation process.

Naturally Jung's unorthodox views about religion opened him to criticism from theologians, who resented his trespassing on their territory. He disagreed totally with fundamentalist points of view, where people held that their own particular brand of belief represented absolute truth. Jung tended more towards the Gnostic view that it was knowledge that counted, rather than faith. He cautioned that whenever dogma takes over, humans lose sight of whatever spiritual insights they had in the first place. Jung felt it was necessary for him as a psychologist to explore this important area of the human psyche in as much depth as possible and so he also made in-depth studies of some of the Eastern religions.

Hinduism

In the Hindu faith there are many gods and goddesses, who all originate from an original creative force called Brahma. Each god or goddess symbolically represents a different divine aspect – such as Vishnu the creator, Shiva the destroyer, or Krishna the god of love. Unlike in the Christian tradition, the shadow side of the divine is openly portrayed.

Jung found the physical postures of yoga helpful for calming the mind and he was fascinated by the symbolic process of spiritual transformation described in the yogic texts. Once again he found a description of the archetypal process of separation and eventual rebalancing of opposites, just as he had in alchemical texts. He saw the physical and meditative processes of yoga as a useful means of relaxing the ego's grip over the unconscious, so that the individuation process could get underway. But he cautioned Western people not to go too deeply into the more obscure practices of Yoga, warning that Western minds are not usually properly prepared and that he felt total psychosis could result.

Although he was impressed by the Hindu religion and yoga, Jung could not accept the ultimate goal, which is *samadhi* – the total absorption of the Self into the divine. He argued that such a state would be logically impossible, because if there is no Self, then there is no consciousness, so who can be experiencing samadhi? In any case, he was not at all happy with an ultimate goal that seemed to represent a total escape from reality. This seemed to him to be pointless and he believed instead that each of us is in the world for a special purpose, which is known to the Self and which it is our task to discover. The goal of Jungian analysis was to help people towards wholeness and to function more fully in the real world.

Buddhism

The goal of Buddhism is to attain an inner state of enlightenment, once again detaching oneself from the physical world and the endless chatter of the psyche. Jung saw parallels here with psychological therapy, where the aim is to alter conscious awareness and so achieve a higher spiritual state.

Jung was particularly interested in *The Tibetan Book of the Dead* – a sort of travel guide for the departed soul. This tied up with other texts that he had discovered; for example, in Ancient Egyptian mythology there is also a *Book of the Dead*. He had explored similar themes when he wrote the *Seven Sermons* (1916) and once again he was struck by the archetypal nature of the teachings that he found cropping up in different cultures. In other Buddhist teachings, he found more vivid archetypal imagery, such as the 'jewel in the crown of the lotus', which he saw as another mandala-like symbolic image for the Self.

Buddhism appealed to Jung because:
* it is up to each person to follow their own path to enlightenment – there is little emphasis on dogma and faith;
* the answer to spiritual growth is seen as lying within – there is no external deity as such;
* the spiritual teachings and meditations are helpful for training the mind towards concentration.

Nevertheless, he also found that there were drawbacks. In Buddhism suffering is seen as an illusion from which one can ultimately escape through attaining enlightenment. Jung disagreed, saying that suffering is real and unavoidable. We can only overcome suffering by living through it and analytical psychology can help us to do that. Also, withdrawal from life is in itself a form of repression – a denial of the shadow – and as such would tend to produce an opposite swing eventually.

Finally, in Buddhism there is an endless cycle of reincarnation, where the individual is born and dies and is born again. The only escape from this dismal trap is through enlightenment. Jung says that this is no good for the Western mind, which needs to feel that it progresses towards a goal and has a purpose in its existence.

After travelling extensively in the East, Jung was eventually drawn back to study Western teachings. He realized that the study of Eastern religions had been important to him, but that it was only a part of the path that would bring him to his goal. He compared the Eastern way of thinking with that in the West and concluded that:

* Western man is mainly extroverted, finding meaning in external objects and looking for meaning in the 'real world' – consciousness in Western man is too detached from the unconscious;

* Eastern man is mainly introverted and looks for meaning within the self – in Eastern man, the tendency is for consciousness to merge completely with the unconscious.

Jung came to realize that meaning was both without and within. He had discovered that both traditions had their own strengths and drawbacks. Neither point of view was completely right nor completely wrong. This insight shows a move towards balance and maturity within Jung's own psyche – an integration of the two sides of his personality that had troubled him for so long.

Changes in Christian thinking

Jung came to believe that Christianity was of central importance to Western man, but it needed to gain new insights in order to answer the spiritual needs of modern people. For example, he felt that there was an imbalance in the doctrine of the Trinity, which sees God as having three aspects – Father, Son and Holy Spirit. Jung felt that this idea did not acknowledge a feminine aspect to the divine. Gnostic teaching had added a 'fourth term', as an attempt to incorporate the hidden and mysterious feminine side.

In 1950 the Catholic Church announced a new doctrine – the Assumption of the Virgin Mary – which decreed that she was taken straight up to heaven, body and spirit, when she died and didn't have to wait for the Day of Judgement like the rest of us. Jung saw this new doctrine as very important because he felt that it acknowledged an archetypal psychological need. Ordinary people had always shown this need in the way that they regarded the Virgin as a comforting, motherly person, whom one could pray to in times of need. She had definitely been venerated all along, even though she wasn't 'officially' divine. People had visions of her and Jung points out that she often appeared to children, suggesting that the collective unconscious was at work.

Jung believed that the study of religion was very important in giving us insight into the workings of the unconscious. He stressed that when he spoke of 'God' he referred to the 'God within'. Whether or not God exists as a separate external entity was for Jung a pointless and unanswerable question. But he believed that it was essential for people to have a spiritual dimension in their lives and that numerous neuroses arose because people overlooked this aspect of their being. People tend to focus on the narrower aspects of life, such as work, marriage and success, but all the while they stay unhappy because they restrict themselves spiritually. Jung saw spirituality as being vitally important to the achievement of wholeness in the human psyche.

10
Jung the visionary

Jung's influence has extended worldwide, making him one of the greatest thinkers of the twentieth century.

* His ideas about the collective unconscious and archetypes have given us new insights into the human psyche.
* His interest in dreams has expanded our understanding of the unconscious.
* Many of his ideas about personality have become part of everyday thinking.
* His fascination with mythology, religion and the paranormal has encouraged people to open up new thinking about spiritual psychology.

Jung used various therapeutic approaches, particularly:

* exploring symbolism in dreams and fantasies;
* amplification of symbols by exploring archetypal connections;
* free association, following trains of spontaneous connected thoughts;
* active imagination, using methods like drawing, painting, drama or writing;
* balancing of opposites in order to achieve greater integration in the psyche.

Jungian analysts are trained worldwide and there are many institutions devoted to expanding his ideas.

Travels

Jung travelled a lot during his life in order to learn about cultures that were different from his own. He visited North Africa more than once, and discovered abundant archetypal presences there: for example, he described the rising sun as being like a vast and powerful god. There were strangely synchronous events too – for example, on arrival at Sousse, he was astounded to see a sailing ship with two lateen sails that he had once painted.

Jung was struck by the way time seemed to slow down more and more the further he travelled into the Sahara. He described an encounter with a figure all swathed in white and seated on a black mule whose harness was studded with silver. This man rode by without offering any greeting, but his proud bearing and the sense that this person was somehow wholly himself, struck Jung as a stark contrast to the average European, who was characterized by a driven attitude and suppression of emotion. He concluded that the great scientific and cultural achievements of Western culture had been gained at the expense of intensity of living, forcing down into the unconscious much that is real and life-giving.

In New Mexico, this point was again brought strongly home to Jung by a Pueblo Indian chief, who graphically described the typical white man's face as cruel, staring and driven. He thought the white men were mad, because they thought 'with their heads'. Jung, surprised, asked him what he thought with himself, and the man indicated his heart – 'we think here,' he said. The Pueblo people had a strong belief that their religion was of benefit to the whole world, because they worshipped and encouraged the sun on its daily course across the sky. Jung concluded that this gave the people a sense that their lives were cosmologically meaningful: it was this deep sense of connectedness that had been lost by so-called civilized Western man.

Jung also visited Equatorial Africa and found a timeless world that had existed even before there were any people to know that it was there. Seeing this, Jung suddenly grasped the cosmic meaning of consciousness – man was like a second creator. In observing the world and being consciously aware of it he gave it objective existence, and so man was indispensable for the completion of creation.

In 1937, Jung visited India. He realized that here, as in many of the other cultures he had visited, people still lived in the whole body and had not retreated to live only from the head as they had in the West. While he was in India, Jung dreamed that he had to swim to a castle on an island off the coast of Britain, bringing the Holy Grail back to its home. For Jung, this dream was a timely reminder that he needed to return to focus on his own people and culture. India was not his goal – it was simply a part of the road that was carrying him closer to his goal.

Jung and psychotherapy

Jung emphasized that every person has a unique story to tell, some aspects of which are hidden in the unconscious. It is the unfolding of this life story that provides the pathway to individuation: a lifelong process that we all need to go through. Jung always patiently talked with people and listened to them in order to really understand their unique problems. He laid less emphasis on childhood experiences than other psychoanalysts had done – for him the person's life *now* was the most important aspect. He always stressed that the spiritual aspect of human psychic experience was of vital importance, encouraging people to realize that they are not isolated beings, but part of a great mysterious whole.

Unlike many other psychotherapists of his day, Jung sat face to face with his patients, and encouraged them to see him a human being, not just as a doctor. However, outside the consulting room he tended to be formal and polite, setting a little distance between himself and his client. He enjoyed helping people to explore their inner worlds, but he was not always interested in his clients' outpourings – one woman who came to see him dissolved into copious tears during every session and he dealt with this by reading the newspaper!

Jung believed that many people became neurotic because of a split in their psyche between the modern and the primitive. Deprived of the mythical truths of their ancestors, and cut off from the world of nature, they developed a huge gulf between the ego and the unconscious. In being helped to close this gulf a person can begin to achieve healing. Jung emphasized that he never claimed to understand a person fully – a person's inner world was their own territory and, as such, it had to be respected. Not only that, but inner growth is hard work and nobody can do this work for somebody else. Unlike analysts from other schools, Jung always stressed the importance of feelings, saying that it is not possible to achieve healing through working only in an analytical way 'in the head'.

One of Jung's most important pupils was Barbara Hannah (1891–1986). Born in England, she travelled to Zurich to meet Jung and stayed in Switzerland for the rest of her life, working as a psychotherapist and teaching at the CG Jung Institute. She wrote many books developing Jung's ideas. Another major follower of Jung was Marie-Louise von Franz (1915–98). She was a founder of the CG Jung Institute and wrote widely on many subjects including psychotherapy, dreams, alchemy, fairy tales and personality types. Jung's lover Toni Wolff also became an analyst, but she published very little, preferring to concentrate on patients.

Key aspects of Jungian analysis

The system of psychology that Jung developed over the years provided him with a useful map of the psyche and gave structure to his therapy sessions. He used various approaches to finding his way into a person's inner world.

Symbols

Jung encouraged his patients to talk about their dreams and fantasies and to explore their symbolic content. These symbolic messages provided clues as to what was going on in the person's unconscious and helped to bring issues into conscious awareness.

Archetypal messages

Many symbolic messages that emerge from the unconscious are archetypal in nature. Jung often worked with these symbols in a constructive way, seeking possible connections with symbolism in myth, folklore and religion, in order to arrive at clarification and enhanced meaning.

Association

Given an original image or idea, Jung would encourage the patient to follow a train of spontaneous connected thoughts. He believed that these were always meaningful in one way or another, and might uncover unconscious complexes.

Active imagination

Jung encouraged people to explore symbolism emerging from the unconscious in creative ways such as drawing, painting, drama or writing. This active imagination process brings the person back to a playful, child-like state that allows the unconscious to express itself more freely.

Balancing of opposites

Jung frequently emphasized the process of balancing of opposites, which is necessary to achieve a healthy integrated psyche. Once two conflicting opposite trends are brought into consciousness the tension between them can be resolved. A third state, representing a new, healthier attitude, can emerge. Jung called this third state the 'transcendent function'.

Criticisms of Jung

Like all great thinkers, Jung has had plenty of critics. Some of them have accused him of being domineering and egotistical, determined to collect devoted admirers in the academic world. Others have suggested he lived off his wife's fortune and was a womanizer – sour grapes perhaps! And, as we have already seen, many dismissed him as an unscientific, mystical thinker, immersed in a fantasy world.

Some have accused Jung of anti-Semitism: this accusation first arose in the early 1930s, when he became president of the General Medical Society for Psychotherapy, which was based in Germany. This was just at the time Hitler came into power, and people were being forced to conform to Nazi ideas. Jung was well aware of the dangers of the ideology of the Society becoming too one-sided, so he worked to alter the balance of membership, which had previously been predominantly German. He saw this new balance as being important not only to allay people's fears, but also to protect the German people from what he saw as an increasing spiritual isolation.

Jung resigned from the Society in 1939 and, by this stage, he was becomingly increasingly and openly hostile to the Nazi regime. His books were banned in Germany and destroyed elsewhere in Europe; at one point, once he was on the Nazi blacklist, he had to flee from his home in Zurich to safety in the mountains. Later, various documents came to light that showed that he had played a major part in advising Jewish friends and helping them to escape to England and the US. Accusations of Nazi collaboration still occasionally get levelled at Jung, but one has only to read what he has to say in his books to see that this has more to do with lucrative and sensational journalism than with the truth. Jung was interested in healing people and encouraging them to grow as individuals rather than in dark power and dictatorship.

Jung was always very popular with women and he was a pioneer figure in promoting the idea that we all have a masculine and a feminine aspect. Theoretically, he supported women and wanted them to have equal rights and make their own way in the world. Nevertheless, he was a man of his times in many ways and his attitude was sometimes rather patriarchal and paternalistic.

Jung's psychology has sometimes been attacked for encouraging people to concentrate mostly on themselves – critics say that he does not give enough attention to relationships with others. However, Jung argues that it is not possible to separate the relationship with the Self from the relationship with others: we cannot hope to relate well to others until we can see ourselves clearly.

Into the future

For Jung, life was a sacred journey with meaning and purpose. His interests were very wide-ranging and he wrote extensively on many different subjects. Above all he was a psychologist and analyst, and it is this aspect of his work that most people come to first. His analytical method gradually strips away built-up defensive layers of the personality until we are able to see our true selves. The goal is to achieve a wider, fuller consciousness, less dependent on ego. This new consciousness is no longer totally egocentric, obsessed with its own petty needs and endlessly using unconscious ploys to cover up its inadequacies.

Certainly Jung himself was not a perfect being, but this only makes him more human – like all of us, he had his shadow side. But whatever he was like as a person, it is certainly true that his influence has extended far beyond his private work as a psychologist, making him one of the greatest thinkers of the twentieth century.

* His ideas about the collective unconscious and archetypes have given us new insights into the history of the human psyche.
* His lifelong interest in dreams has expanded our understanding of the mysterious world of the unconscious.
* Many of his ideas about personality, such as introversion and extroversion, have become part of everyday language and understanding.
* His fascination with mythology, religion and the paranormal has encouraged people to open up new thinking about spiritual psychology.
* Many modern forms of psychotherapy have roots in his ideas.

Jung's charismatic personality has inspired many people and taught us to look deeply within ourselves and to begin to accept ourselves for who we truly are. Ultimately, this is a spiritual journey – one that Jung saw as being essential if mankind were to have a future. It is this conscious awareness and fulfilment of one's own unique being – the individuation process – that is the pathway and the goal of Jungian analysis.

Synchronous events surrounded Jung right up until his death. The day he died, 6 June 1961, his friend, writer and visionary Laurens van der Post had a dream of Jung waving goodbye. The same day Barbara Hannah discovered that her car battery had suddenly run down completely. His death was followed a few hours later by a violent storm, during which lightning struck his favourite poplar tree by the lake. In what was probably his last 'big' dream, he saw a huge round stone on a high plateau. At its foot were engraved the words 'And this shall be a sign unto you of Wholeness and Oneness.' His journey through life was complete.

Notes